THE NIGHT TRAIN

AND

THE GOLDEN BIRD

&The Night Train
The Golden Bird

PETER MEINKE

University of Pittsburgh Press

Published by the University of Pittsburgh Press, Pittsburgh, Pa. 15260
Feffer and Simons, Inc., London
Manufactured in the United States of America

Library of Congress Cataloging in Publication Data

Meinke, Peter.
  The night train and The golden bird.

  (Pitt poetry series)
  I. Title.
PS3563.E348N5   811'.5'4   76-43966
ISBN 0-8229-5280-7

Thanks to the National Endowment for the Arts for a fellowship in creative writing for
1974–75, during which many of these poems were written, and to Hamline University for
appointing me poet-in-residence during the fall of 1973, when I wrote "Lines from Neu-
châtel" and several other poems.
    Some of the poems in this book first appeared in *Cafe at St. Marks, Carleton Miscellany,
Epos Anthology, Florida Quarterly, Inlet, Konglomerati, Mad River Review, Motive, New
Orleans Review, Red Clay Reader, South Florida Review, Southern Voices,* and *Twigs.*
"Bones in an African Cave" copyright © 1966 by the Antioch Press. First published in the
Antioch Review, vol. XXVI, no. 2. Reprinted by the permission of the Editors. "Blue Girl"
and "Cheerios" originally appeared in *Cosmopolitan* magazine. "Because" reprinted from
The Massachusetts Review, © 1961 The Massachusetts Review, Inc. "The Night Train"
and "Lift a Glass to the Memory" first appeared in *New Collage Magazine,* vol. VII, no. 3.
"The Patient," "Old Man River," "Morocco," "The Magic Kingdom," "Chicken Un-
limited," "this is a poem to my son Peter," "you stand in isolation," "Origins," "The
Monkey's Paw," "Ode to Good Men Fallen Before Hero Come," "Because," "Vegetables,"
"Surfaces," "Poem to Old Friends Who Have Never Met," "When I with You," "Father
kept an anchor," "Teaching Poetry at a Country School," and "Dear Reader" reprinted by
permission of the *New Republic,* © 1970, 1971, 1972, 1973, 1974, 1975, 1976, The New
Republic, Inc. "Gramma" first appeared in *Poetry NOW.* "At the Ojubo Shrine, Nigeria"
won first prize in the 1976 Writer's Digest Poetry Contest and was first published October
21, 1976, in the *St. Petersburg Times.* "Charleston" and "Cinnabar" were first published
in *Southern Poetry Review.*

The publication of this book is supported by a grant from the National Endowment for the Arts in Washington, D.C., a Federal agency.

for Jeanne

CONTENTS

II. The Golden Bird

I. The Night Train

THE NIGHT TRAIN

In its closed compartments
the fingers of suicides curl loving
around pens and knives
carving out on paper and skin
the poem of their lives
taking the night train to nowhere
rattling the tracks at 90 miles per hour
their futures unrolling behind them
each agony, each cry, repetitive
as railroad ties, statistically boring

The train compartment is the perfect thing
better than the cancer clinic with
its pale green walls and plastic chairs
old copies of *Better Homes* and *True*
the opaque rippled glass, showing also green
like the walls, like patients chewing their lips
fingers twitching for forbidden cigarettes
better than the $6 motel room with
its two dim lamps and revolvable TV
the large mirror before the flimsy bed
the Gideon Bible, the roaches in the bath
the people in these places already dead
their fingers drum the drumroll of their wake
on train compartment windows, when they take
their lives it is the right place
this closed anonymous world inside a train
a nothing sort of place; for god's sake
get on with it: there's nothing much at stake

THE PATIENT

disease has expanded my horizons
and pain
spread the good word

since I've been sick
I feel close to the blighted things of nature
(I myself am a blighted thing of nature)
　　burnt oaks
　　gutted houses
　　　(for surely houses are as natural as beehives)
　　broken foxes lying by the highway

　　bugs crawl along the rims of my glasses
　　my body pocked with spiraled holes
　　like those punched in butter
　　in each hole something　　moving

hooked on disease (it gives
meaning to my life)　　I wriggle wormlike
around the pain and God
is the large-mouthed bass circling
below me

THE POET TO HIS TONGUE

The day they cut my tongue out
I spit a lot of blood but
basically was pleased:
I'd nothing to say, no one heard
and the damned thing was diseased anyway:
redwhite cankerroses bloomed
words burned like houses
a sentence filled a room with dead birds

I don't believe in God
but I believe
God was trying to tell me something:
shut up.

Then, I took my tongue home
not wanting to lose it (him?) completely
and curled that infected rascal up
stuffed him in a bottle of Jim Beam
(which he favored when alive)
& stuck it on the windowsill
over my desk where I nightly
in silence nod to my ex-flesh
where it spins still, turning neat
as the moon
filters through dreams & whiskey
& sometimes strange music seems
to come from it, a strain
unnatural and familiar
that speaks of love and pain
& hope & pain
& pain & pain &

but maybe it comes from the beerjoint across
the street

OLD MAN RIVER

no longer what he used to be
nor am I though I never was
what he used to be but
I'm scared of livin'
and tired of dyin'
while Old Man River's
just a sweet ole sentimental song but still

when the sky is low
and the sun hangs red
above the riverbed
and the willowbranches bend
where the river runs
you think well

Some diseases are incurable
but we don't know which ones
so we keep going upstream
downstream
all around the townstream
Old Man River he keep
us rollin' along

MOMIA

The scars on her arms prove
she was sucked dry by witches
so now   bone-bag   scarecrow
she haunts the churches of Merida
ghostly beggar
singing her own circle of hell
invisible city
of dead lovers and children
afraid to look in her eye
When she was young
her breasts full
she led men into the jungle
left them there to die

MOROCCO

Marrakech, Meknes, Fez, Casablanca
names on a map deep in our minds
minarets & almond trees laying long shadows:
cobblestone streets under keyhole arches
shine in the darkness like broken teeth

The soul is a camel
with a hump full of sentimental images
clumping across real deserts
seeking the perfect oasis that is no mirage
(no one has ever reached it)

Marrakech, Meknes, Fez, Casablanca
the walled cities are truly beautiful
and corrupt, in the center they decay
like molars, the pain is spreading
a white path for revolution

What shall happen to the almond trees?
they shall be burned with bazaar & babouche
their seeds shall burst underground from the heat
green shoots will spring up
their bitter leaves nibbled by lost camels

WALLS

I

may God grace me with words
to sing my vision
as he touched Caedmon, that young cowherd
centuries ago
near Hadrian's great wall
in the cattle-stall, in the straw
when the words came in the night
like cows to the barn breathing & warm
praising God's starbright creation
this middle-earth
our desolate dreamfilled world
spinning through space
dandelion seed
blown across the pasture
where fattening cattle stand
motionless in the morning mist

II

in the dark cell of a dead leaf
lurk cities & forests
shelves of unwritten books

indestructible combinations

let us say a man, or a fox
lived near Langres 400 years ago
and habitually skirted the old wall
& knew it well, & loved it, & then died

endless transformations

so that
when I turn a corner
when you step off a train
& we enter a scene already completely known
it is only new to our edges
we are linking up with our center
breaking down the wall

dark illuminations

III

it would all be so simple
if only the waves would roll in smoothly
up to the great wall the children sit on
or the black rocks stay in their toothy row
or the laughing gulls with their hangmen's hoods
would quietly pick up the clamshells to drop on the rocks

but swollen with malice the waves reach ragged arms
for the children, the rocks keep moving around
like giant crabs; and the gulls keep picking up
rocks they think are clamshells
& dropping them on the rocks but they
always miss and pick up another & drop it
& miss with the terrifying patience of the insane

and there is always one child missing

IV
trying to meet myself halfway
moving toward the moon
I celebrate well, tunnel, bog & owl
Sister
I am thinking circle
Mother
I proceed oblique
Father
I'm kicking down the walls
to let in hag & temptress
they stream in like moonlight
like the odor of decay
endless transformations
of serpent & dove, pig & fox
we exchange skulls and drink
the mooncalled blood
my eyes are spiders spinning a holy web
in which all creatures sleep
for 7 years
and then are born again
indestructible combinations
they dance along the parapet of my wrist
dandelion seeds
down the steps of my fingers
against the white moons of my nails
dark illuminations
tracing in the sand below the walls
"In the beginning everything
started all over

CHARLESTON

the high walls of Charleston
never smile or make noises
like the motels of Miami
New York's neon monsters:
at night the walls of Charleston
grow taller; behind them
the houses lean together
gracefully, whispering
across wisteria and azalea
the old stories beautiful and false

    the bones of slaves
    turn beneath the streets
    pushing up bricks relentlessly
    beneath the buicks
    and ancient cadillacs

the pillared porches and the flying stairs
vibrate in shadow, tuned to music
of memory and disaster: rats on the eaves
rats in the attic
chewing up the brown photographs
the albums, the polite letters
that touch you strangely
the crinoline and abandoned handkerchief:
the rats are absorbing the culture
they bow to each other
by chimneys they
lean elegantly on the drainpipes
their grey coats shine
in the moonlight sleek
fat with garbage

    in the restaurants the young heirs
    carefully divide the china
    the dark portraits

by day
the flat sun burns the grass
the sons of the cotton brokers
teach art to pimply boys
who don't give a rat's ass
but the beauty is real
behind the music
behind the wall
like the white arc
of infrared rainbows
Charleston
great oak
riddled with ants
smothered by Spanish moss
thrusting its magnificent
dead silhouette
against the setting
suns

DWARVES

strung out on caffeine & tobacco
those out-of-date sustainers
shaking fingers hover above
the typewriter electric
trying to remember, trying to pull out
last night's dream, or last year's
wristblood racing the clock

shadows in the room like dwarves
darting along the bookcase, the piano
keys press down of themselves
invisible fingers making dwarf music
the room fills with bridges
with tunnels, the sound of picks
and dripping water, someone
laughing hysterically where is
my father, my mother what am I
doing here in this echoing darkness following
this music and the soft sound of wings

and there, waiting at the end
the dark at the end of the tunnel
and the high laughter of a hundred dwarves

THE MAGIC KINGDOM

Why do so many fat people go to Disneyworld,
haunches lapping over the little seats
in the Grand Prix or Mr Toad's Wild Ride?
Does one feel weightless there, reality displaced
so you soon begin sniffing plastic roses
and they really smell like roses but better?

20,000 Leagues Under the Sea ("E" coupon)
we stare out our portholes at fake fish on wires,
the flat surface 6 inches above. Our kids ask,
Are the bubbles real?   Who knows?

The Master's dead: behold his Haunted House
at the top of Liberty Square (the orange map);
as Mickey said, he had a mind like a steel
mouse—and the smile of reason that
warmed the clean columns of Monticello
fades into the flat grin
of a mechanical Cheshire cat. Pink
pilgrims shoulder in the squares
cuddling the comic relics of infancy. In Fantasy-
land Mike Fink performs
an unnatural act on Dumbo the Unresisting
or is the heat getting me?

And yet
to stand in the middle of that circular movie
(admission free)
and see the crowd lean far to the left
feeling they're taking a curve
was (shall we say)
educational.

CHICKEN UNLIMITED

Today is our 16th anniversary
the suet anniversary, everything
turning to fat
At my side as I drive home squats Chicken Unlimited
the 16-piece box: we have four kids
sometimes I think we eat too much chicken
it makes us want to kill each other

Our house is surrounded by oaks, azaleas
thriving on 6-6-6 and chicken bones
Chicken Unlimited is afraid of being alone, is
beautiful:
"scarlet circles ring your eyes
your bill as black as jet
like burnished gold your feathers gleam
your comb is devil-red"
I think the sky is falling

Chicken Unlimited constantly breaks his neck
against an invisible shield
he can't get at the flowers

He is ambitious: wants to be president
wants to fuck the Queen
he wants to be Johnny Carson
he takes extension courses at night
but doesn't know what to think

I'm stuck in the traffic on 12th street
the man behind is honking like a crazed goose
I think he's after Chicken Unlimited

My son comes home bloody
"If I run, they call me chicken,
if I fight, he beats the shit out of me"
That's right, I say
that's the way it goes

Chicken Unlimited is jumping on my chest
its beak rakes my face
I think it wants to kiss me
I think it wants to eat me alive
I say, Chicken Unlimited
your kisses taste like wine
but I'm too old for this sort of thing

In the sky the constellations realign
the Big Dipper points to Chicken Unlimited
the rings of Saturn are grain
for its celestial gizzard
the sky is surely falling

One of my dreams is playing centerfield
in Yankee Stadium: C.U. is at bat,
smashes a towering drive I race back back
over the artificial grass
but the ball becomes an egg becomes
a bomb
as I/we crash together at the monument

Chicken Unlimited worries about his input
he wants to make it perfectly clear
but it still comes out cluckcluck
cluck cluck
he is weak on his relative pronouns

Daughter (age 9): Where do babies come from?
Mother: Why, from inside a woman.
D.: Yeah, how'd they get there?
M.: Well, let's see, how to explain it . . .
D.: Yeah, the old chicken in the bun, right?

Right.

Chicken Unlimited has such energy!
Like our kids
chicken tracks in the sooty snow
Still stuck in this insane traffic
man behind still honking me deaf
wanting to get home to my wife, my children
this crazy urge to stick my head
out the window, and yell
Compliments to the Chef!

GRAMMA

My grandmother was like your grandmother:
she hung in there, played pinochle
and watched the Dodger games
until they took her to the hospital
and when I visited her (home from school)
I embarrassed the family
by vomiting in the corridor,
all those tubes, in the nose, in the arm
of Gramma, who was tougher than I.
And when she came home to die,
after four days of not eating
asked for a half grapefruit and died
in Mother's arms. No one had seen her
get up, but in the closet were folded
neatly her burial clothes.
Old Gramma, she loved
heavy chairs, big trees, her old house.
A little lady, she demanded
little, gave much and
enjoyed what was available.
There's a lot to be said for hanging in there.

(untitled)

this is a poem to my son Peter
whom I have hurt a thousand times
whose large and vulnerable eyes
have glazed in pain at my ragings
thin wrists and fingers hung
boneless in despair, pale freckled back
bent in defeat, pillow soaked
by my failure to understand.
I have scarred through weakness
and impatience your frail confidence forever
because when I needed to strike
you were there to be hurt and because
I thought you knew
you were beautiful and fair
your bright eyes and hair
but now I see that no one knows that
about himself, but must be told
and retold until it takes hold
because I think anything can be killed
after a while, especially beauty
so I write this for life, for love, for
you, my oldest son Peter, age 10,
going on 11.

(untitled)

You stand in isolation like the first bloom
of some enchanted plant. Around you lies a field
of sullen energy where strange creatures
only seen by you move in slow motion
with majestic beauty, their sharp hooves
spraying broken glass like water, the field
covered with the stained glass of old
cathedrals. And you are trapped in this magic
terrible land you more than half desire. I think
I hear you crying, I think you think
no one can reach you. Don't cry, look;
I'm taking off my shoes.
I'm coming in.

THIRD CHILD: JUNE 11, 1962

Third child, it's crowded in my house
and heart. But here, I'll make a place
for you to lie, and sleep and cry.
Your world is crowded too: the mouse
is trapped, the kitten drowned, and dogs chase
dogs away, no place to stay,
no place to rest. The predatory
order of our days sharpens the claws
of children as they grow. I know
the center has not held, the glory
prophesied has died stillborn because
there was no room, there is no room . . .

No room for Gentile or for Jew;
East and West grapple in the dark
tied in one bag, cramming a flag
down one another's throats. And you,
third child, will seek in city parks
the room to run, but when the sun
sets it is not safe. You'll ask,
But why, why should I be afraid?
And I will say, Gretchen, the way
of man is dark, his face a mask
his outward life a grim charade
concealing narrow rooms, revealing
nothing. . . . Of course, I won't say that,
I'll say, Don't be afraid.
There's nothing to fear. I called you here
because it's bedtime, and that's that.
It's time you knelt beside your bed and prayed.

AT THE OJUBO SHRINE, NIGERIA

In the jungle near Ilê-Ifê clay hands
reach out through vines above the brown river
ruled by Ogun god of iron whose huge fingers crush
rock and ebony like the small bones of children.
Green silence magnifies everything: shrill
chatter of putty-nosed monkeys, the heartbeat in my ribs
as I press your letter tightly to my side.
Only an artist totally possessed
could have carved these writhing figures out of clay
that the relentless rain already is unwinding.
And I who have traveled too far from you
call on the powers of darkness with all my strength
CALL ON THE POWER OF OGUN WITH ALL MY STRENGTH
to bring us both together in the light
far from this fierce place where humans carve
mad messages to the popeyed gods

BONES IN AN AFRICAN CAVE

Bones in an African cave
gave the show away:
they went violent to their grave
like us today.

Skulls scattered on the ground
broke to the brain;
the missing link is found
pointing to Cain.

Children in the street
pry up the cobblestones.
Old instincts repeat
in slender bones.

To my violent son,
beautiful and strong,
caps in his polished gun,
I hymn this song.

Grow tall and gay and wild,
strong-voiced and loud;
be proud of the fierce blood
that won't die out.

All things repeat
after the floods and flames:
new boys play in the streets
their ancient games.

ORIGINS

Humble origins are   American
as violent pie:
centerfielders sprout in ghettos,
scholars blossom on Appalachian ranges;
Morrison the birdwatcher bred pigeons
on his tenement roof.

Now they have discovered psychedelic mushrooms
growing in manure in Florida
(the cows become self-conscious from the crowds).
A truly American story
and the lowly cowturd has taken its place
beside the log cabin
as the sacred fount
of inspiration and the dazzling dreams of youth.

THE MONKEY'S PAW

When the war is over the bones of the lonely dead
will knit and rise from ricefield and foxfield
like sea-things seeking the sea, and will head
toward their homes in Hanoi or Seattle
clogging the seaways, the airways, the highways
climbing the cliffs and trampling the clover
heading toward Helen, Hsueh-ying, or Mary
when the war is over

When the war is over Helen, Hsueh-ying, or Mary
and lonely women all over the world
will answer the knock on the door like that insane story
and find on their doorstep something they used to hold
in their arms, in their hearts, in their beds
and that something will reach out and crumble
and the eyes cave back in the head
when the war is over

When the war is over curses will mount in the air
like corbies, to flock over capital cities
and flutter and hover and waver and gather
till white buildings turn black beneath their cloud
and then they will drop like bombs, talons
zeroed in on the dead hearts still walking around
on the ground with memos in their briefcases
when the war, when the war is over

ODE TO GOOD MEN FALLEN
BEFORE HERO COME

In all story before hero come
good men from all over set forth
to meet giant ogre dragon troll
and they are all killed every one
decapitated roasted cut in two
their maiden are carted away and gobbled like cupcake
until hero sail across white water
and run giant ogre dragon troll quite through

Land of course explode into rejoicing
and king's daughter kisses horny knight
but who's to kiss horny head of slaughtered
whose bony smile are for no one in particular
somewhere left out of story somebody's daughter
remain behind general celebration
combing her hair without looking into mirror
rethinking life without Harry who loved his porter

I sing for them   son friend brother
all women-born men like one we know
ourselves   no hero they no Tristan
no St. George Gawain Galahad Sgt. York

they march again and again to be quartered and diced
and what hell for them never attempt to riddle
I'm talking about Harry Smith caught in middle
who fought pretty bravely for nothing and screamed twice

ABSENCE

lamplight lies in a ring
of dead moths, the bed fills
with broken wishbones

o my lifegiver the radiator stands frozen
in stony silence, the sofa drains
in a pool of red; ashtrays spill their ashes
beercans loiter in corners

you could come back & touch this all to life:
the wings of the chairs
flutter as you go by

the hands of the clock are chained
by your absence, the hours chopped
like logs & dumped on my doorstep
Love, the door is open

CINNABAR

Poison flows from the rock in Sierra Morena
even in winter, even the coldest day
(the years slide, we slide with the years)
somehow it reaches us
from the air, from the sea
from the great fish near the ocean floor
Quicksilver slips through our veins
sticking between tongue and brain
like a pebble in a door.
In Sierra Morena the townspeople stutter
the Mad Hatter is mayor
Belladonna his fair lady
It is half-past one, time for dinner
and he asks
Why is a raven like a writing desk?
No one answers, there is no answer,
outside the crows declaim
the daily news with raucous voices
The green benches by the flower-beds
sag with old folks shaking in the cold,
the flower-lady selling tight posies
of deadly nightshade
croaks like a magpie in the afternoon.
By night, our home huddles in the dark
the room spinning in firelight
the four figures of the cuckoo clock
dance and turn, children wrestle on the floor.
Wounded and different, Jeanne & I
(the years slide, we slide with the years)
drink the vermilion bittersweet wine
swallow the poison from the East
thinking, as we forgive and love;

knowing, as we love and forgive:
grammatically speaking, at the very least
like all things lit by the winter sun
a raven and a writing desk are one.

LINES FROM NEUCHATEL

I. Café du Pont

La vie est difficile, monsieur,
Madame Nicoud, our concierge,
said, mopping our kitchen floor
one afternoon. *Mais oui, vraiment*
I answered like a horse's ass
feeling stupid staring at my typewriter
while the sweat poured over
Madame's square red face.
Her thick & battered legs bulged
as she knelt on the old tiles
prodding me to write something, anything.
So I type: *La vie est difficile, monsieur.*

❋

I look out the window. Michel
is working in their small vineyard
on the sloping ground of Neuchâtel.
Across the lake the Alps are hid in mist,
the Alps are always hidden in the mist.
We know they're there.
Michel's wife left him for a captain
in the air force, an American. *Les américains
ont toujours beaucoup d'argent, m'sieu,*
he tells me. I try to look poor.
We *are* poor.
So why don't I work, *eh m'sieu?*

❋

Swiss houses are turned backwards.
First you go through an iron gate
ten feet high with wicked spikes, then
walk around it, up steep steps
to the heavy entrance
facing a blank wall holding back
the foothills of the Jura mountains.

Monsieur Nicoud keeps the steps immaculate,
picks up each leaf straying from the vine.
He'd like to catch them before they fall.
Except the Nicouds, Michel, & us,
nobody ever comes.

❋

On Saturday night we all go out
together, along the narrow street
below the Suchard factory until, winding upward,
past the vineyards and the apple trees,
we see the tiles of the lower city
now black against the lake.
Bonsoir m'ssieurs 'dames: Jocelyn sings
her greetings at the door of the Café.
We eat, the food is good. We drink.
We drink to each other.
We drink to the Alps.
We know they're there.

II. Hôtel du Truit

When we came up the Gorge that Sunday
John & Jeanne & I, the children running ahead
disappearing, appearing in the tall grass
we were dizzy from the rivercooled wine
so the hotel seemed at first a mirage:
we were in a movie, we were stars
the children's bounds turned suddenly slow motion
and silent, the colors washed
pale as we held hands and approached
the tables under the ancient trees.
A painting by Seurat: Swiss families
clustered in the checkered shade, wine-
bottles winked on colored tablecloths —
and then the sound turned on, Swiss music,

laughter, hands held out in welcome
glasses filled, *pour les américains*
and we sat, on our sunshine holiday
at this crazy hotel in the woods
in the middle of beautiful nowhere
and almost forgot
the brooding darkness of America,
of all countries, the violence
of which we formed a part
and watched the children
under this neutral sky
John & Jeanne & I

III. Hôtel Lion d'Or

Taking the tram to Boudry was an adventure:
we could get off, along the way
at Auvernier, Colombier
little hamlets each with its café
some *spécialité* to set it off
and if one happened carelessly to cough
a little blood upon the tablecloth
why, in a minute it was whisked away.

Or we could get off between-towns, where the river
flicked shallow over stones, and in the shadows
speckled trout hid trembling, like leaves in air
and at the end, the old clock tower over Boudry
abandoned now, but lovely, and the clock of course
still working perfectly
this being Switzerland where life
ticks on correctly and the chimes
all come on cue. Thank you,
we *are* marvelous, and,
eating our escargots like good bourgeois

we sometimes shake our heads and forks to think
of poor Marat, bleeding in his bathtub,
born improbably in this very room
how many years ago?

IV. Cabaret Voltaire
The fathers of all the pretty children
keep in the closet nearest the front door
a rifle oiled & waiting:
when the Russian wolf
leaps over the eastern Alps
boom   boom   boom
when the German dog
crosses the Bodensee
ouah   ouah   ouah
Switzerland will be ready
like a child doubling a fist
against his Daddy.

> *The swans of Lucerne swim round & round*
> *the tourists throw them pfennigs & pounds*
> *& the swans they gobble them down them down*
> *the swans they gobble them down*

O Switzerland where is your Dada now?
Where is your boomboomboom your
rosy Anna Blossom?
In the closet Dada's in the closet
where your little triggers fatten
like commas around a stiff proposition
where Freud forever sucks Napoleon's fingers
and there the lederhosen grin like clamshells
there the albino dwarf chewing on chicken bones
there the drain where Marat's blood
continually swirls, the closet never lies

like pretty girls, there pale parasites gnawing
something like money ouah ouah ouah
départ des trains suicides
boomboomboom
we follow where the red-eyed rabbits lead

V. Café Vue des Alpes

When the fog dropped swiftly
over the ski slope
all the pretty children
were lost among the trees.
Hallooo we cried Halloooo
but the fog swallowed our words
and hung them from the branches
pointing down, no human sound
could give direction there
and we stumbled blindly over
the treacherous snow, parents & children
lost and wandering
like leaves in a swirling pool.

The only sound
that somehow slipped the fog
and cut through thinly in irregular places
was music from some loudspeaker,
or some café, that could be heard
clearly for a while and then would go
and come again from somewhere else—
a lively tune, an accordion perhaps,
and slowly, in the fog, children & parents
began heading erratically toward the music
all of us separately, yet together
like leaves in a running stream;
at least we thought so,
being unable to see.

NEUCHATEL SWANS

dine wanly on pretzels
which they hold in their beaks
like firemen carrying children

my children swim in cold green water
diving off stones below
the splayed feet of swans unafraid
of anything, anything

they do not fear the blue shadow
turning circles deep in the water
there are no sharks in lake neuchâtel
but what the hell is that shadow

they have heard of the black swan
who eats geraniums they have seen
the tall gates of the houses
close like beaks

but it is all a story
scare me daddy, tell me another story
and one day there he is, son of a gun
there on the horizon sails the black swan

immense and satisfied, white
geraniums in his mouth
preening toward the children who swim out

little pink fingers

BECAUSE

because
death is so lovely
so self-possessed
we have a tendency
to jump the gun
before the molecule's dissolution
the final bad breath

because
death is a communicable disease
only childless men
can commit suicide
without setting a time bomb
in the fragile cabins
of their children

and because
death is so attractive in the abstract
a rest
freedom from pain
we should bite our lips to remember
it doesn't taste good
and it leaves a stain

II. The Golden Bird

THE HEART'S LOCATION

all my plans for suicide are ridiculous
I can never remember the heart's location
too cheap to smash the car
too queasy to slash a wrist
once jumped off a bridge
almost scared myself to death
then spent two foggy weeks
waiting for new glasses

of course I really want to live
continuing my lifelong search
for the world's greatest unknown cheap restaurant
and a poem full of ordinary words
about simple things
in the inconsolable rhythms of the heart

EVERYTHING WE DO

Everything we do is for our first loves
whom we have lost irrevocably
who have married insurance salesmen
and moved to Topeka
and never think of us at all.

We fly planes & design buildings
and write poems
that all say Sally I love you
I'll never love anyone else
Why didn't you know I was going to be a poet?

The walks to school, the kisses in the snow
gather, as we dream backwards, sweetness with age:
our legs are young again, our voices
strong and happy, we're not afraid.
We don't know enough to be afraid.

And now
we hold (hidden, hopeless) the hope
that some day
she may fly in our plane
enter our building   read our poem

And that night, deep in her dream,
Sally, far in darkness, in Topeka,
with the salesman lying beside her,
will cry out
our unfamiliar name.

CHEERIOS

you are what you eat & I
I am a sexmad wheatgerm
floating in holes of cheerios
stamped out of Kansas farmland
where in late August
the All-American sun
drives ripe farmgirls into barns
and shadows as pitchforks
are abandoned like Neptune's
trident while he rolled in the springs
with Ceres, seeds exploding
everywhere, pine cones and
pomegranates, ears of corn
popeyed with heat
bunches of grapes swollen
in the wagon while we
danced & sang & drank
& ate and the god laughed
& chanted, crying
gobble it all in excess of
the minimum daily adult requirements
screw hunger
look longer
live younger

VEGETABLES

"Just because they can't say anything
doesn't mean they don't hear you coming";
tomatoes, in particular, feel pain
thin girlish skin and
seeds quaking in jelly at the first prick
and carrots, shrieking silent
like St. Bartholomew as you peel them
from foot to head: they feel,

they feel. Disemboweled peas

slide into tumbrils, dizzy
with air, beets bleed on the
sinkboard, celery wilts with its heart
in our hands, squash
turns pale on our tables
and when you pick up the knife
and walk across the kitchen, shoeheels softly drumming
even the coarse hydra-headed potato hears you humming

SURFACES

       darling
you are not at all
like a pool or a rose
my thoughts do not dart in your depths
like cool goldfish
nor does your skin suggest petals
you are not *like* anything (except perhaps
my idea of what you are like

I think you are like
what our children need to grow beautiful
what I need to be most myself)
when the moon comes out I do not think of you
but sometimes you remind me of the moon:
your surfaces are unbelievably real

This is how I feel about you:
suppose
on the surface of a rippling pool
the moon shone clearly reflected
like a yellow rose
then
if a cloud floated over it
      I would hate the sky

HAPPY AT 40

STOP: if you're racing at night
over cobblestones winking like turtles
to meet an important party in 15 minutes
when an ancient winedark man reels out
of a one-eyed bar with parachutes
sagging from the ceiling and croaks
A tugboat captain
is a tough captain
skip the bus, forget about the party
follow him into the bar if
you want to be happy at 40

LOOK: if you're in Paris or Munich
or Barcelona drinking beer with a whore
who weighs over 200 pounds
and is not pretty
when you see a friend of the family's
from your home town approaching
be certain you stand up and say Mr. Barnes
I'd like you to meet
my friend Marie who is showing me
this marvelous city,
if you want to be happy at 40

LISTEN: lies are all around us
it's only sporting, life is tricky
like poetry, lies, lies abound,
testing you, setting you up
for an occasional truth
like this:
if you see a woman leap over a hedge
marry her on the spot
take her forcibly on the greensward for
your life depends on it
if you want to be happy
at 40.

POEM TO OLD FRIENDS
WHO HAVE NEVER MET

When I'm not wishing I could find a unicorn
I wish all my old friends knew each other
The very least they deserve
is the pleasure of each other's company
We'd go down by the river
and the rocks would hum
with this rich collection of men & women
They would look around and see themselves
no longer isolated
no longer points in the darkness pointing nowhere
but as links in a magnificent chain of
impossible flowers
girdling the world, and their talk
(they are all talkers)
would burst like spray in the sunlight

and I would smile, saying nothing
with a bottle of beer in my hand
and a small white bird banging in my heart

BLUE GIRL

because you wore blue yesterday
today I am in love with everything blue
The blue books on my shelves smile at me:
TEN GREEK PLAYS and CONVERSATIONAL FRENCH
Que j'adore le bleu!
Bleu, blau, azul, azzurro . . .
words popping like blueberries in my mouth
My indigo wastebasket too pure for use:
applecores fly out the window
When I close my eyes
visions of violets and sapphires blow them open
bluejeans & bluebells, blueback trout leap from the walls
No good telling myself
it's only a wavelength of energy
so many radiant millimicrons zapping my eyeballs:
one man can handle only so much blue
I'm writing this with a red ballpoint pen
using blue only for punctuation
at my age even the semi-colon is risky
but I hate being careful
I feel like ending it all
Looking for you
I'll dash out in this blue October day
and let those bright blue chips
                              fall
                              where they may

WHEN I WITH YOU

When I with you so wholly disappear
into the mirror of your slender hand
grey streets of the city grow roses
and daisies, the music of flowers
blooms in our voices, the eye of
the grocer flares like a candle

Hey my heels click like dice on the sidewalk
riverboat gambler I'm loaded & lucky
spinning my wheels as I walk with my lady
queen of my heart who suits me entirely
till the bones of your fingers tap on my cheekbone
and open my eyes to the clocks in the mirror

SUNDAY AT THE APPLE MARKET

Apple-smell everywhere!
Haralson McIntosh Fireside Rome
old ciderpresses weathering in the shed
old ladders tilting at empty branches
boxes and bins of apples by the cartload
yellow and green and red
piled crazy in the storehouse barn
miraculous profusion, the crowd
around the testing table laughing and rolling
the cool applechunks in their mouths
dogs barking at children in the appletrees
couples holding hands, so many people
out in the country carrying bushels
and baskets and bags and boxes of apples
to their cars, the smell of apples
making us for one Sunday afternoon free
and happy as people must have been meant to be

EROTIC POEM

I am too embarrassed
to write an erotic poem for you:
suppose my mother read it, or your mother?
What would they think
if I listed the various parts
of our anatomies
that work so well together?
What would they think
of this position or that place,
the look on your face just before,
the feeling I have just after?
I think I shall have to wait
until our mothers are gone

and by then it may be too late.

In the meantime,
baby,
you turn me on.

DISTANCES

Some distances cannot be crossed; like
Zeno's arrow you can only go halfway at a time:
there remains a remoteness, a shadow thrown
across an almost infinitesimal line:
a separation.
I am usually glad there is a distance between us:
it gives me somewhere to go.
But now, you are 467 miles away
as the crow flies, and I think
That's not a bad number: 4 + 6 makes 10,
the perfect figure, minus 7 makes 3,
the holy trinity or the eternal triangle
neither of which interests me particularly
though I am obsessed by numbers.
I also think, That I am not a crow,
and the actual distance from these shores to you
by shipboard, camelback, Greyhound, underground,
is considerably longer. I can remember
there were times when I could not tell
where I ended or you began

My lost pilgrim
the contours of your body defy distances
and cannot be measured by instruments or statistics:
the distance, for example, between your knee and your ankle
is approximately the distance between
the crow's shadow in the evening
and the soft scent of gardenias;
and the hollow of your absence is wider
than the sound of seashells in September

(untitled)

Father kept an anchor in the basement
huge and barnacled
an illuminated text for the children:
This house will stand. Old sailor,
old soldier, he steered through wars
and storming northern seas straight as a die
only to lose his course in suburban New York.

Anchors are made of iron
and so was my father
and though I don't understand what makes things magnetic
so compasses spin like gyroscopes rolling downhill
and a man veers at an ankle or pales at an eye,
he showed me love is varied as shells on the shore

and
though compass and anchor may guide you and hold you in port,
like the flare that illuminates trenches in the smoky night,
like the disease whose rays brighten the fevered eye,
like the bear whose roar brings the wilderness to its feet,
romantic passion is the lodestar of this world.

CRACKING

always pressed against the shell of madness
but which side of the shell am I on?
waver on the verge of obscene words in church
or exposing myself at the st petersburg public library
in the poetry section

sometimes when driving close my eyes count to 10
but nothing ever happens
especially as I tend to peek at about 5
maybe this is normal
to be half-crazy

terrified at the violence within me
that breaks out only in daydreams when I slice
person after person, burn section after section.
what kind of person would dream like that?
friends get upset at my questions

but there are some things that I fiercely want to know
like "What would Dostoevsky think if he were alive?"
and "Exactly when should you prune azaleas?"
and "Where do all the drag queens go
when they're over 45?"

ANGELS DRINK

for JOB

Everywhere
over the spinning world
cognac is evaporating
drifting unseen through the sober air
which accounts for the irregular motion of certain stars
and the high price of cognac

Gentlemen, something must be done:
everyone to his station!

My project is a world-sized tarpaulin
sewn from the skins of aristocratic gerbils
raised entirely on muscadine seeds
all I need now is the zipper
I shall slip it on the world like a magic wineskin
and then

then ladeez & gennelmen
Life will be a Five-Star Holiday!

On Saturday nights I'll give an extra tug
and drops of cognac
will sprinkle the earth
like the tears of intoxicated angels

LIFT A GLASS TO THE MEMORY

John Archibald is dead. Finally. He was
old enough, he lived hard enough.
John, I thought you'd never die,
you talked about it so much.
You'd say, as we sat in O'Gara's,
the 3 o'clock sun slanting through our beer,

What're you young Turks
doing here with an old fart like me?

Something was wrong with your heart:
it hurt like hell, it
never grew a shell but humped
in its bone cage like a baby's tongue
waiting for the right words, the right
poem:

You guys are supposed to be so smart,
What's it all about?

Most people get lobotomies in middle age
to ease the pain. They carve a hole in your head
the size of a judge's fist, reach in and
pull out the garbage: rats & raw nerves,
lust and stinking hopes
and that grinning devil with his unquenchable thirst
and skin like sandpaper
that scrapes you awake
through those long Minneapolis nights

Listen, what do you think of this? Suppose
God's in these bubbles, laughing at our jokes?

John, we loved you because
the pain was so obvious
you never outgrew it
never understood why
things happen as they do.

Well, they do. Fuck it boys.
Have another drink on me.

BUFFALO SKULL

for Leland Cooper

over five thousand years old, they
tell me, muck-brown now and still
frightening with that wide
expanse of forehead and sharp
outcurving horns. And with all
that room in your huge head
the brain was as small as
a stone, packed tight by muscle
and gristle, tendon and white bone.
They say you're extinct now
(the modern breed's horns curve in),
that you snorted and coughed in vain
in that wild prehistoric scene,
failing to impress eternity or
the unsentimental gene . . .

and yet
you impress *me,* you old killer,
and I (living less than a pinpoint
on a geologist's chart) sometimes,
when I feel particularly
insignificant (which is often),
think I would like to leave
in place of my small impermanent heart
your great and powerful skull
in my brown coffin
(around which Homo sapiens cough and grieve).

ELEGY FOR A DIVER

for R.W.

I

Jackknife swandive gainer twist
high off the board you'd pierce the sky
& split the apple of the devil sun
& spit in the sun's fierce eye.
When you were young you never missed,
archer-diver who flew too high
so everything later became undone.

Later everything burned to ash
wings too close to the sun broke down
jackknife swandive gainer twist
can't be done on the ground
and nothing in your diver's past
had warned you that a diver drowns
when nothing replaces what is missed.

Everything beautiful falls away
jackknife swandive gainer twist
muscles drop and skin turns coarse
even skin the sun has kissed.
You drank the sun down every day
until the sun no longer existed
and only the drink had any force.

Only the drink had any force
archer-diver who flew too high
when you were young you never missed
& spit in the sun's fierce eye.
Later everything burned to ash:
everything beautiful falls away
even skin the sun has kissed
jackknife swandive gainer & twist

II

and now I see your bones in dreams
turning & twisting below our feet
fingerbones bending out like wings
as once again your body sings
swandiving slowly through the stone
that sparks your skull and shoulder bones
layer by layer and over and over
you flash through limestone sand & lava
feet together and backbone arched
like an arrow aimed at the devil's heart
the dead are watching your perfect dive
clicking their fingers as if alive
high off the board & the hell with the chances
once again your body dances
anything done well shines forever
only polished by death's dark weather
diver   diver   diving still
now & forever I praise your skill

BYRON VS. DIMAGGIO

Yesterday I was told
the trouble with America is that
these kids here
would rather be DiMaggio
than Byron: this shows our decadence.
But I don't know,
there's not that much difference.
Byron also would have married Monroe
or at least been in there trying;
he too covered a lot of territory,
even with that bum foot,
and made the All-European swimming team
in the Hellespont League.

And, on the other hand, you
have to admit that DiMag played
sweet music
out there in the magic grass
of centerfield.

TEACHING POETRY AT
A COUNTRY SCHOOL IN FLORIDA

It ain't there. Come off it, Rousseau.
The eyes roll inward, the brain coughs
like a motor at ten below

and doesn't start: they're not bad kids.
Too dumb for poetry, and smart enough to know
they don't need it: no one needs it:
not their teachers, nor principal, nor coach
who equates it with queers
and public masturbation
which unfortunately it sometimes resembles
particularly the iambic

But we have to do it because
in the midst of that tangible boredom—
from that stack of pathetic papers—
there is always one you come across
just before turning to drink
with thoughts of murder or suicide—
there is always one who writes
My wings are invisible but brilliant;
they carry me to the dark forest
where the unicorns kneel in prayer. . . .

So. You go on, after a while.
But still, all that effort, so little to show
like that royal palm outside my window going up & up
and up, with a small green *poof* at the top.

J RANDALL RANDLE

J Randall Randle was an undercover
poetry lover   on bottlegreen links
he'd knuckle the pockets of his narky
knickerbockers   duck in the grove by
the 13th hole where he shanked
his Spalding   & pull out the wrinkled
lines on Prufrock   thin & balding

on raindark evenings   walking the dog
he'd snap down the brim of his tan fedora
snap up the collar of his London Fog
& tie the lout to a doctor's bumper
while he read by penlight in alleys
off murderous cobblestone streets
Down by the salley gardens
My love and I would meet

one evening when he returned he found the thread
broken which he had taped over his fake bar and
knew that someone had turned around the false
bottles and had seen his poetry books lined up
like bullets in a belt and 2 weeks later when
Billy Hines casually asked at a party Say Randy
what's a sonnet? J Randall Randle stalked him
home for 14 blocks and shot him iambically kaboom
kaboom between the lines

BECAUSE

Because
everything is by accident
and we are out of control
when most careful
depending on others
to carefully not run us over,
I like a man who laughs loudly,
who swears, and pounds his glass,
and pats the giggling waitresses
as they pass.

Because
we don't know
what will happen to our children
or what happened
to our fathers and mothers,
I like men who love baseball,
who shout at the losers
for not winning, and stretch
with much noise
in the seventh inning.

Because
we are lost and bewildered
with decisions and revisions,
I like men with large appetites,
who belt down hamburgers
and corn on the cob
and whistle popular tunes off tune
on the job.

And because
an old monk
disguised as a young graduate student
once told me (and I believe him),
blessed are the debonaire
for they shall walk in darkness
breathing fresh air,

because of all this
I want to sing,
and dance, and maybe
write beautiful poetry
(though this, too, is chance).

PLOVERS

for V.M.

How can a two-fingered poem catch a plover
in its feathers, piping the sandy beaches
over & over, scuttling stiff-legged skipping
in front of the ripple that rolls
                          and reaches
for the quick feet always four inches
away? What can a poem say:
thick-billed, black-bellied, killdeer, turnstone,
words rolling in front of the wave
or clicking tiptoe across black rocks
like a flock of birds.

Hartley hunted plovers all his life
catching them on canvas one by one—
black-bellied killdeer thick-billed & turnstone—
all kinds, painting them standing, nesting, marching,
hopping, writing poems about them on the back
of his paintings; all kinds, but always hunting
for that rare golden plover that never appeared,
never whistled down the long stretches of shore
from Maine to North Carolina, the bird
that all of God's birdwatchers dream about.

Some day a poem of mine snapping across the
white reaches of blank space just ahead of the
blind sea in which all is lost may swing
around the bend clickety-clack and find
chuckling unaware that golden plover O rare
shining in glorious sunlight unafraid
around its neck a silver clasp with a poem
of Hartley's rolled inside head & back erect
on long quick legs and will run around

over & through it eyes wings beak will be mine
the poem will cradle that bird & protect
and caress those unbelievable soft feathers & frail bone
and will take it all alone to Cape Cod
or Narragansett an abandoned beach
on a rainy day by the cold sea
and there I suppose
will give it back to Hartley & it will be
a feather in the golden cap of God.

DEAR READER

Why don't you write you never
write   each day I check the mail
nothing but truss ads & christmas seals
where are you what are you doing
tonight?

How are your teeth?
When I brush mine blood
drips down my chin
are you happy do you miss me
I will tell you
there is no one like you
your eyes are unbelievable
your secrets are more interesting than anyone else's
you had an unhappy childhood
right?

I will rub your feet they're tired
I'll say Hey
let's go to the movies
just the 2 of us
love

peter

THE GOLDEN BIRD

The mind can't sing a poem without the eye
that, staring inward, changes tree to Tree
with roots and branches in the inner sky.

The world's a place where real birds really fly
into a distance only children see.
The mind can't sing a poem without that eye.

The birds disperse, the stormclouds clash on high
while children watch the wild electric tree
that roots and branches in their inner sky.

The clouds disperse, the children raise a cry
to see a rainbow curving toward the Tree;
the mind can't sing a poem without that eye.

The birds return, the scattered children try
to find the gold that's buried near the Tree
that roots and branches in the inner sky.

The clouds return. Children grow old and die.
The Tree remains, a golden bird nearby:
the mind can't sing a poem without the eye
whose roots and branches touch the inner sky.

PITT POETRY SERIES
Paul Zimmer, General Editor

Dannie Abse, *Collected Poems*

Adonis, *The Blood of Adonis*

Jack Anderson, *The Invention of New Jersey*

Jack Anderson, *Toward the Liberation of the Left Hand*

Jon Anderson, *Death & Friends*

Jon Anderson, *In Sepia*

Jon Anderson, *Looking for Jonathan*

John Balaban, *After Our War*

Gerald W. Barrax, *Another Kind of Rain*

Leo Connellan, *First Selected Poems*

Michael Culross, *The Lost Heroes*

Fazıl Hüsnü Dağlarca, *Selected Poems*

James Den Boer, *Learning the Way*

James Den Boer, *Trying to Come Apart*

Norman Dubie, *Alehouse Sonnets*

Norman Dubie, *In the Dead of the Night*

Odysseus Elytis, *The Axion Esti*

John Engels, *Blood Mountain*

John Engels, *The Homer Mitchell Place*

John Engels, *Signals from the Safety Coffin*

Abbie Huston Evans, *Collected Poems*

Brendan Galvin, *The Minutes No One Owns*

Brendan Galvin, *No Time for Good Reasons*

Gary Gildner, *Digging for Indians*

Gary Gildner, *First Practice*

Gary Gildner, *Nails*

Mark Halperin, *Backroads*

Michael S. Harper, *Dear John, Dear Coltrane*

Michael S. Harper, *Song: I Want a Witness*

Samuel Hazo, *Blood Rights*

Samuel Hazo, *Once for the Last Bandit: New and Previous Poems*

Samuel Hazo, *Quartered*

Gwen Head, *Special Effects*

Milne Holton and Graham W. Reid, eds., *Reading the Ashes: An Anthology of the Poetry of Modern Macedonia*

Shirley Kaufman, *The Floor Keeps Turning*

Shirley Kaufman, *Gold Country*

Abba Kovner, *A Canopy in the Desert: Selected Poems*

Paul-Marie Lapointe, *The Terror of the Snows: Selected Poems*

Larry Levis, *Wrecking Crew*

Jim Lindsey, *In Lieu of Mecca*
Tom Lowenstein, tr., *Eskimo Poems from Canada and Greenland*
Archibald MacLeish, *The Great American Fourth of July Parade*
Peter Meinke, *The Night Train and The Golden Bird*
Judith Minty, *Lake Songs and Other Fears*
James Moore, *The New Body*
Carol Muske, *Camouflage*
Thomas Rabbitt, *Exile*
Belle Randall, *101 Different Ways of Playing Solitaire and Other Poems*
Ed Roberson, *Etai-Eken*
Ed Roberson, *When Thy King Is A Boy*
Eugene Ruggles, *The Lifeguard in the Snow*
Dennis Scott, *Uncle Time*
Herbert Scott, *Groceries*
Richard Shelton, *Of All the Dirty Words*
Richard Shelton, *The Tattooed Desert*
Richard Shelton, *You Can't Have Everything*
Gary Soto, *The Elements of San Joaquin*
David Steingass, *American Handbook*
David Steingass, *Body Compass*
Tomas Tranströmer, *Windows & Stones: Selected Poems*
Alberta T. Turner, *Learning to Count*
Alberta T. Turner, *Lid and Spoon*
Marc Weber, *48 Small Poems*
David P. Young, *Sweating Out the Winter*